It´s time for creativity, distinction and focus

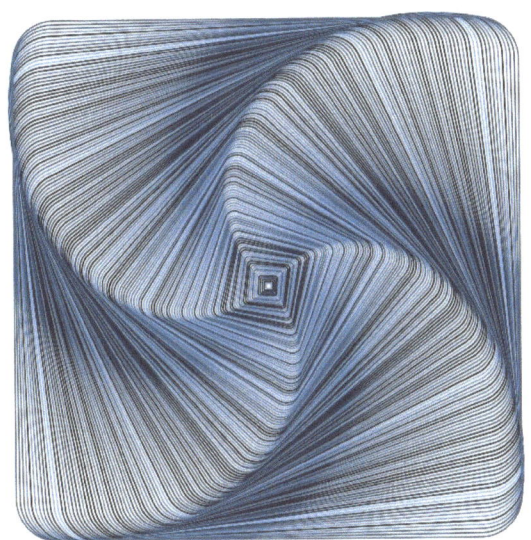

Verry
best
mandala

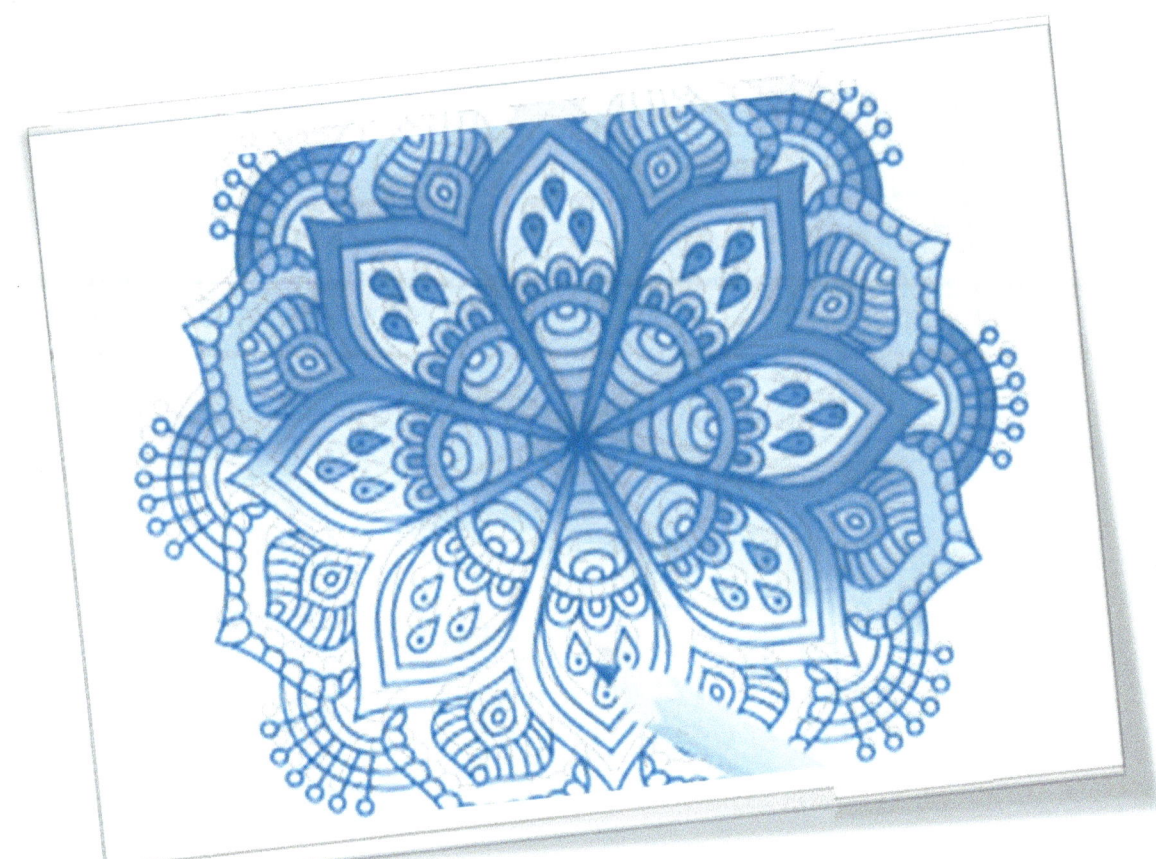

What is a mandala?

In Sanskrit, the word mandala means "circle", and circles are a powerful symbol found in many cultures. We see them in halos, prayer wheels and other religious symbols, as well as architecture and nature.

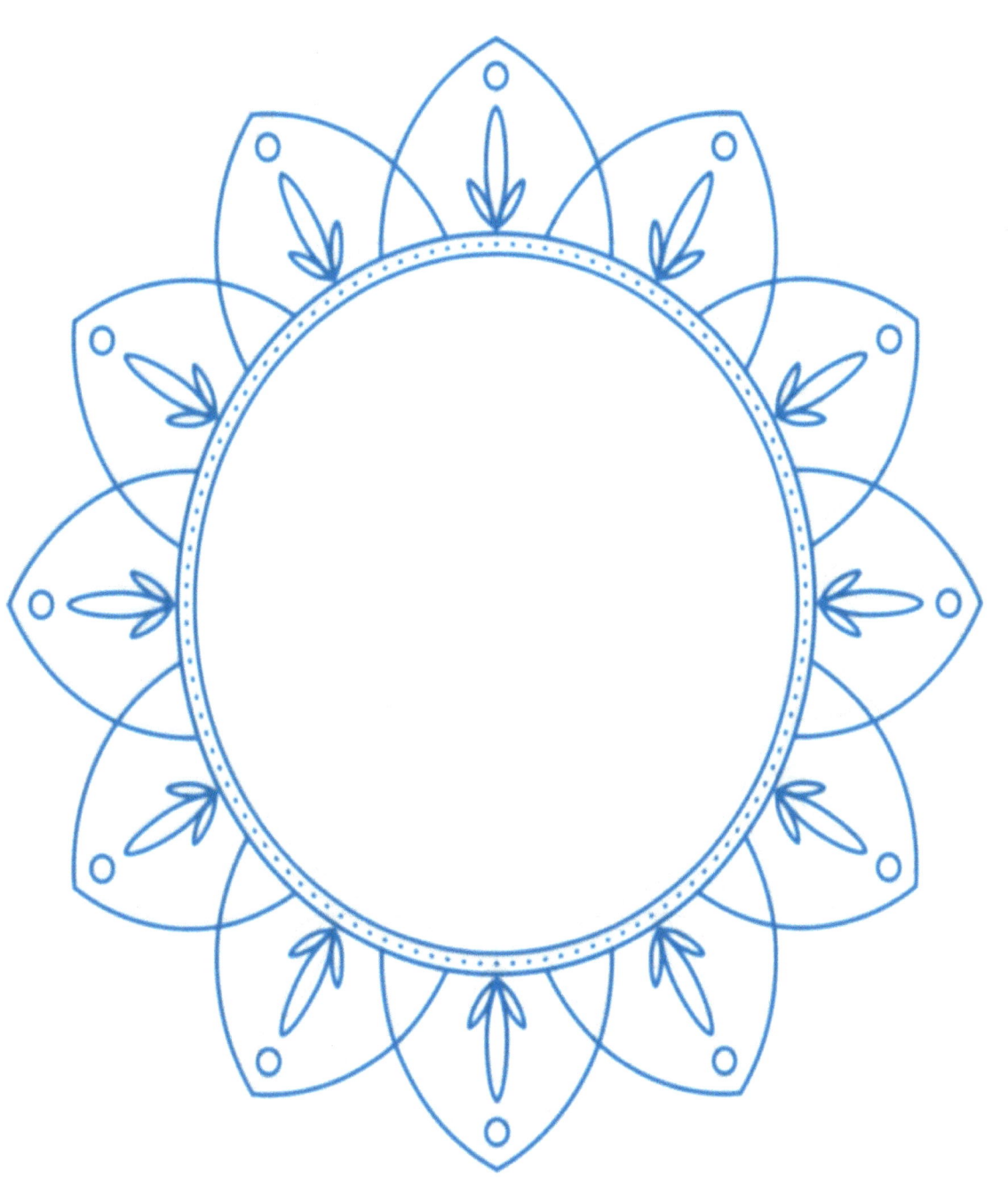

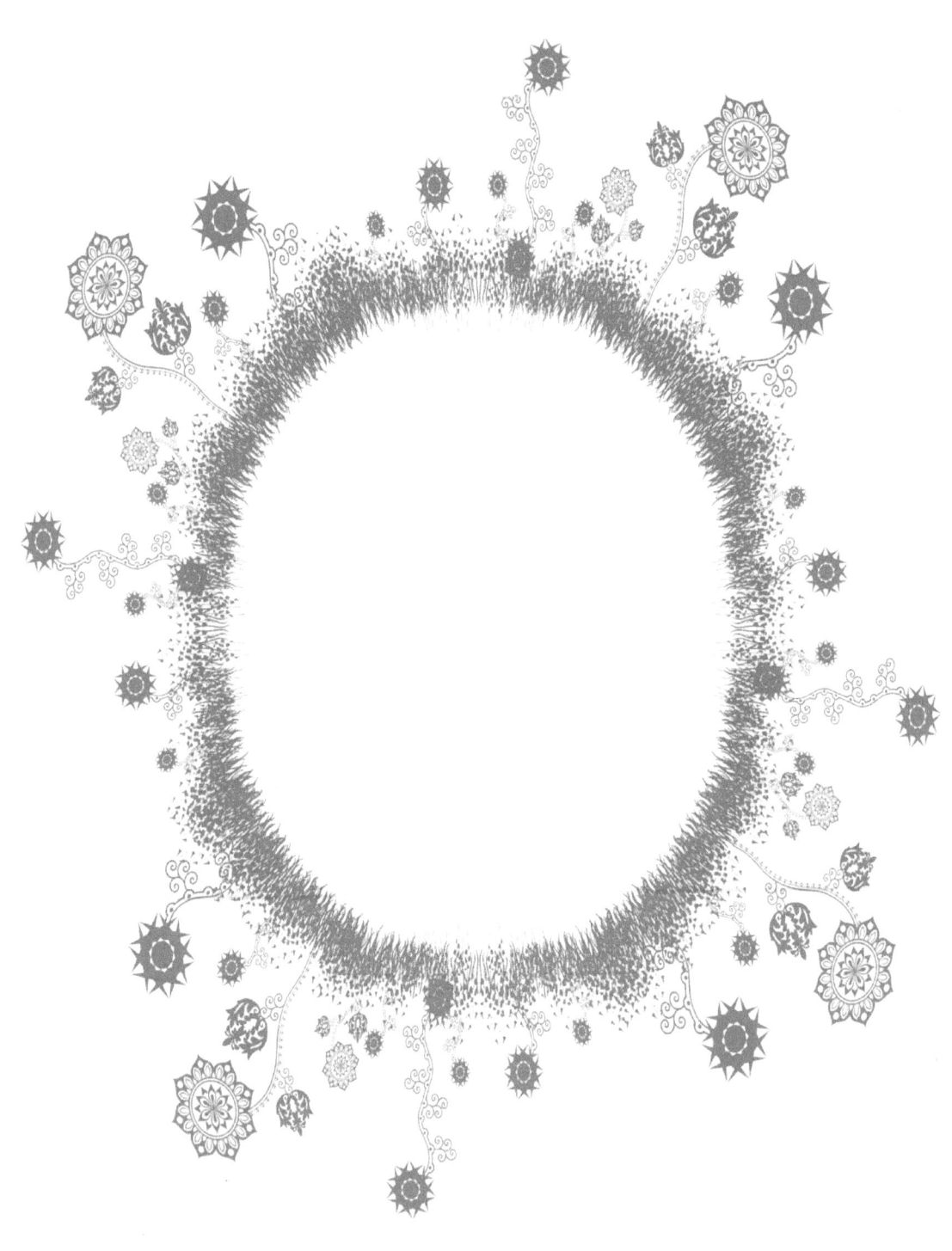

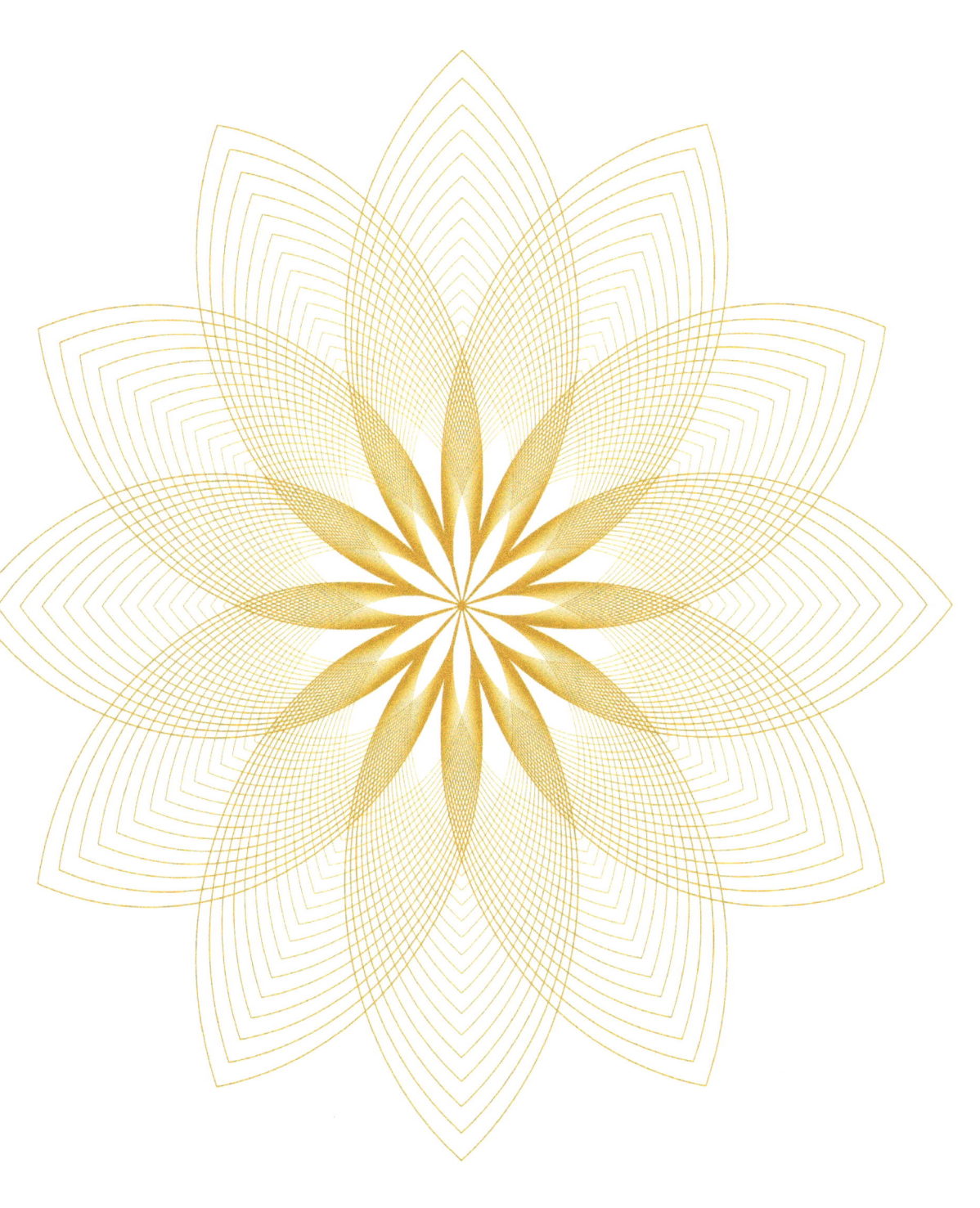

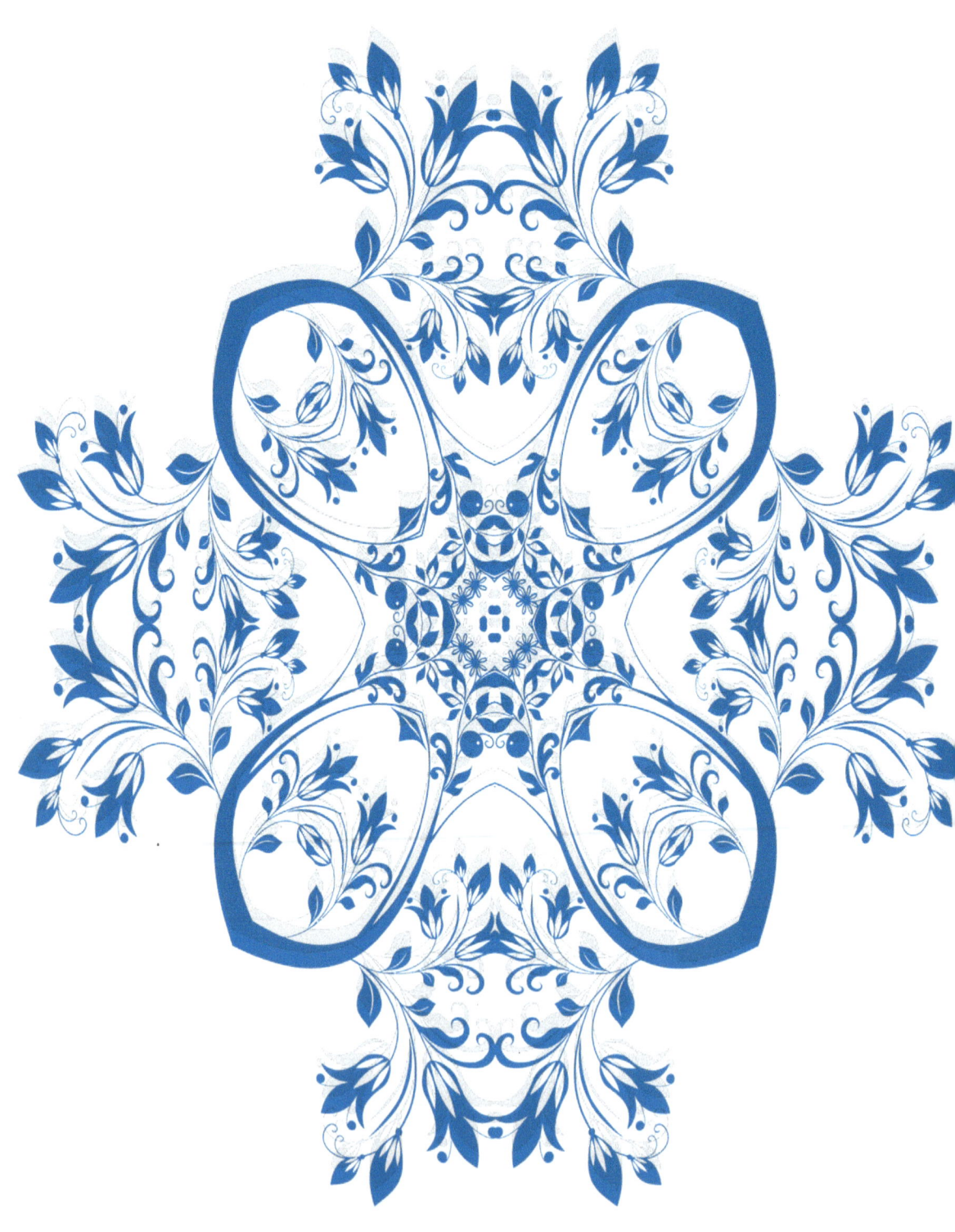

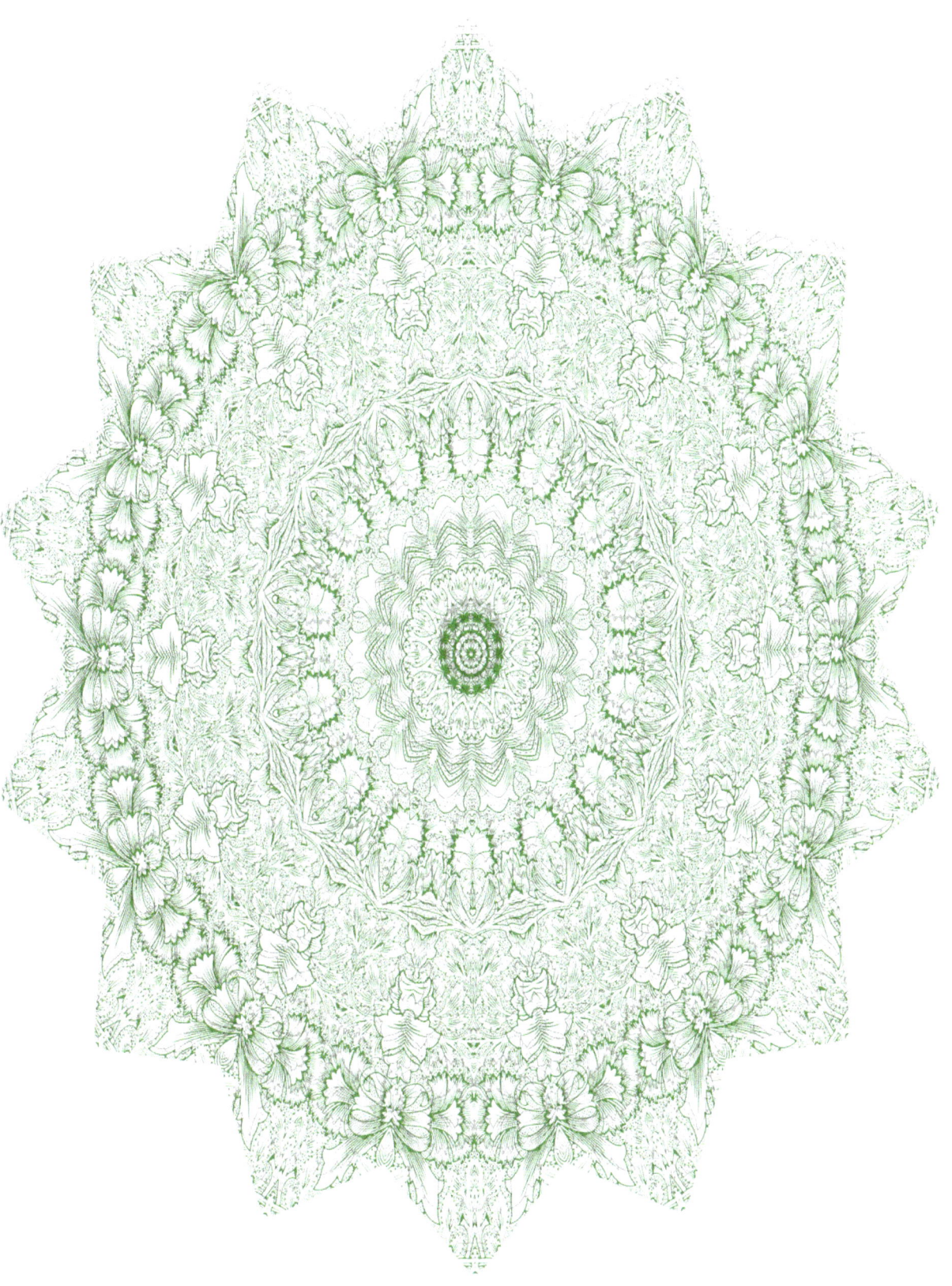

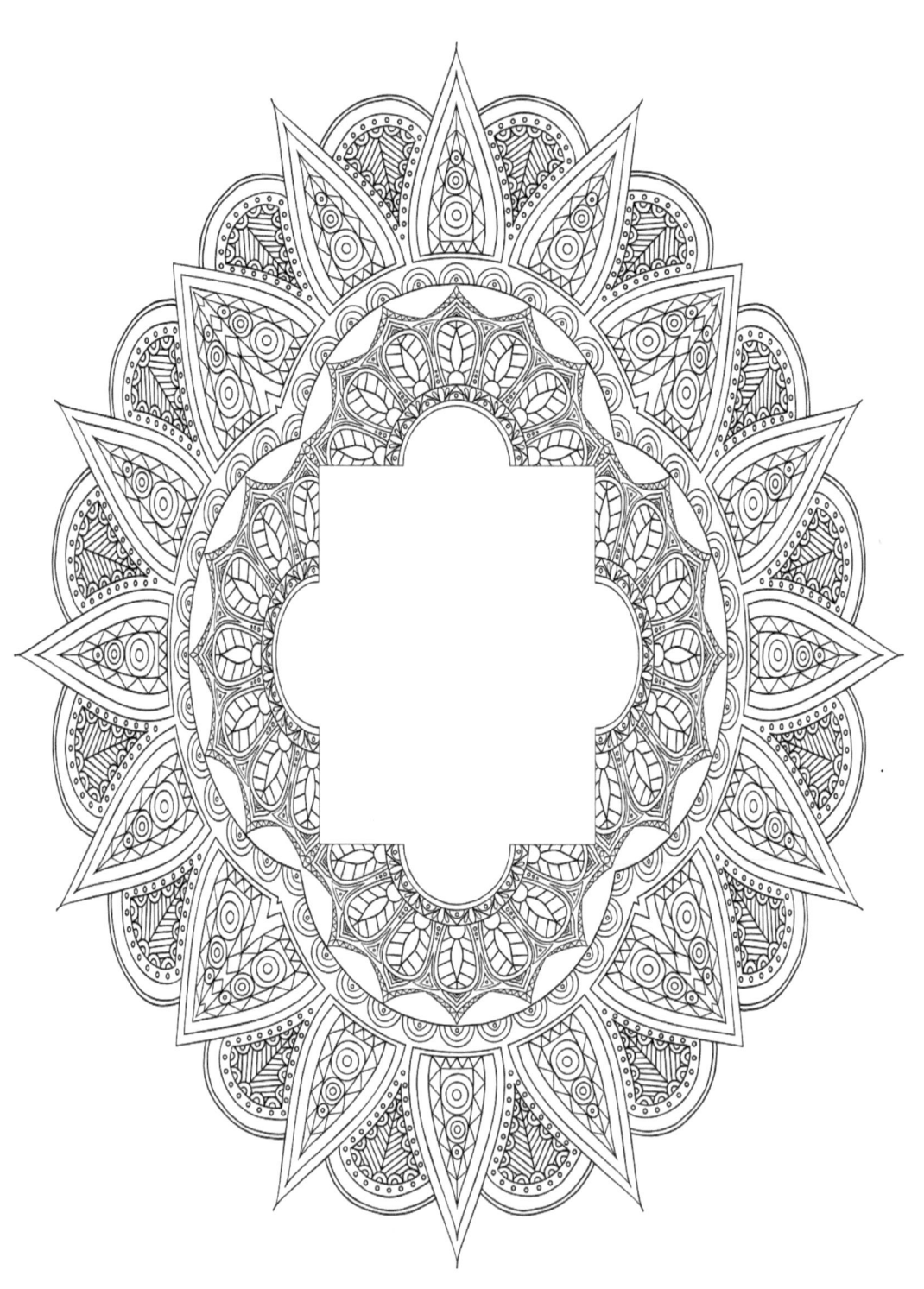

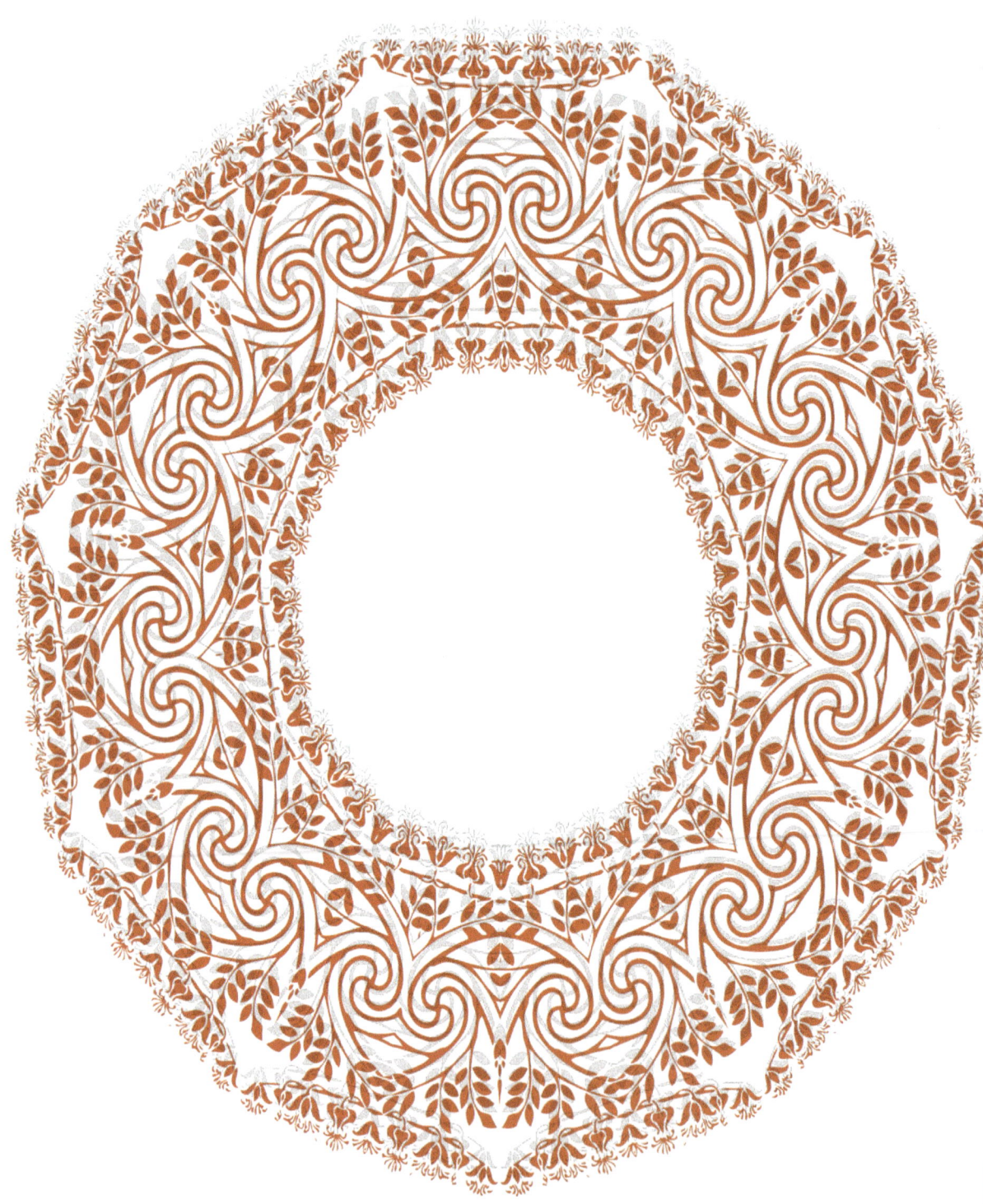

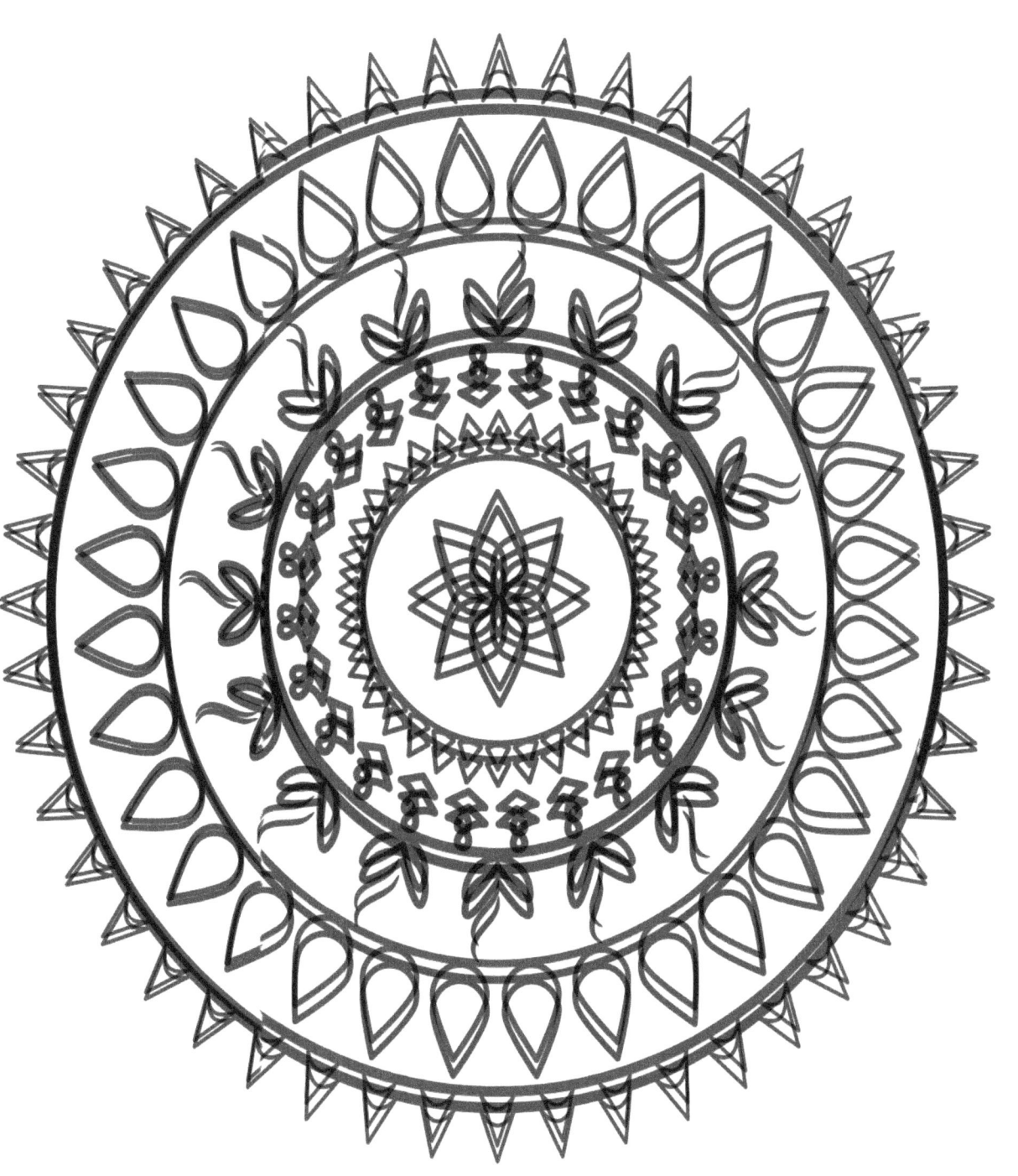

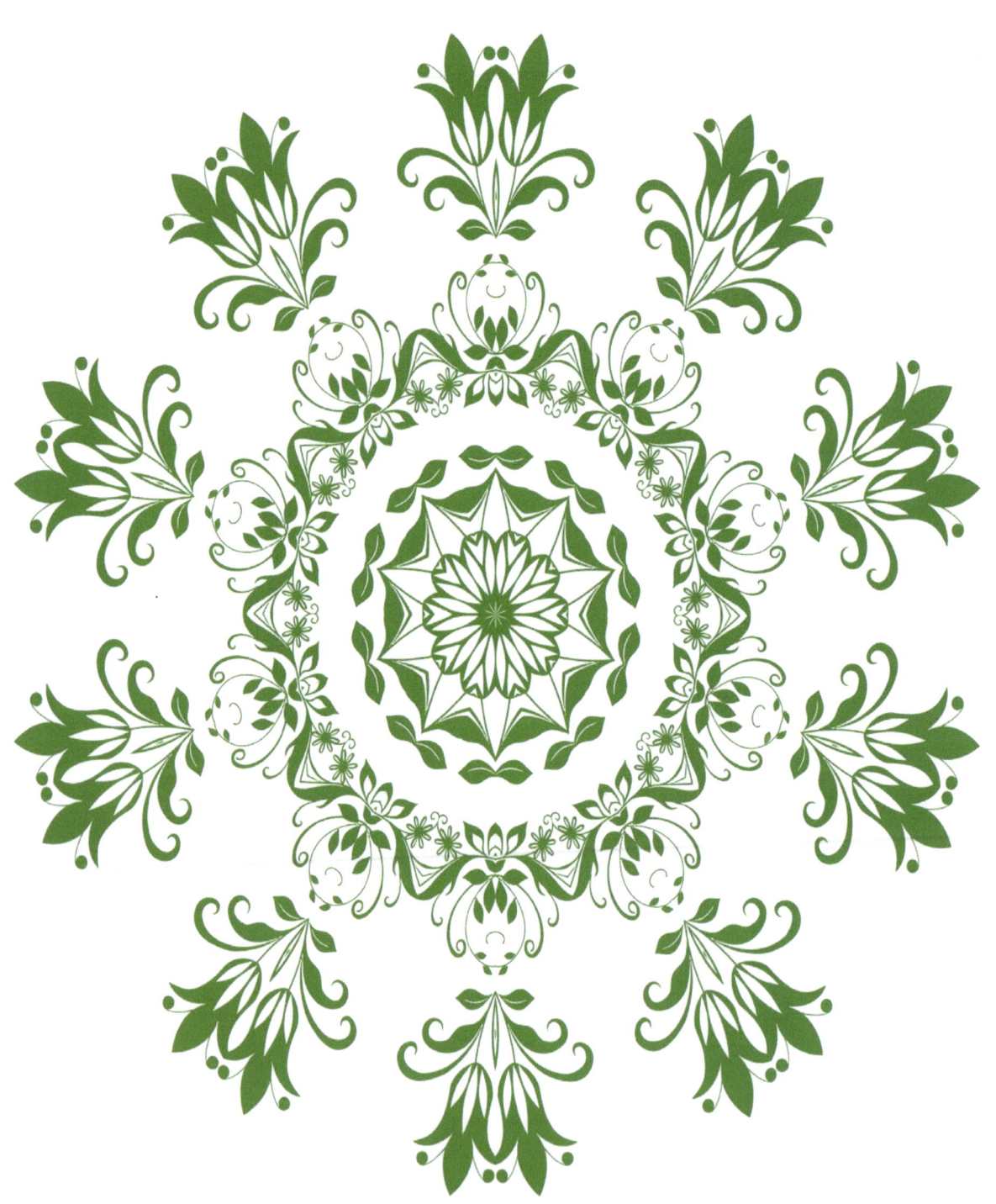

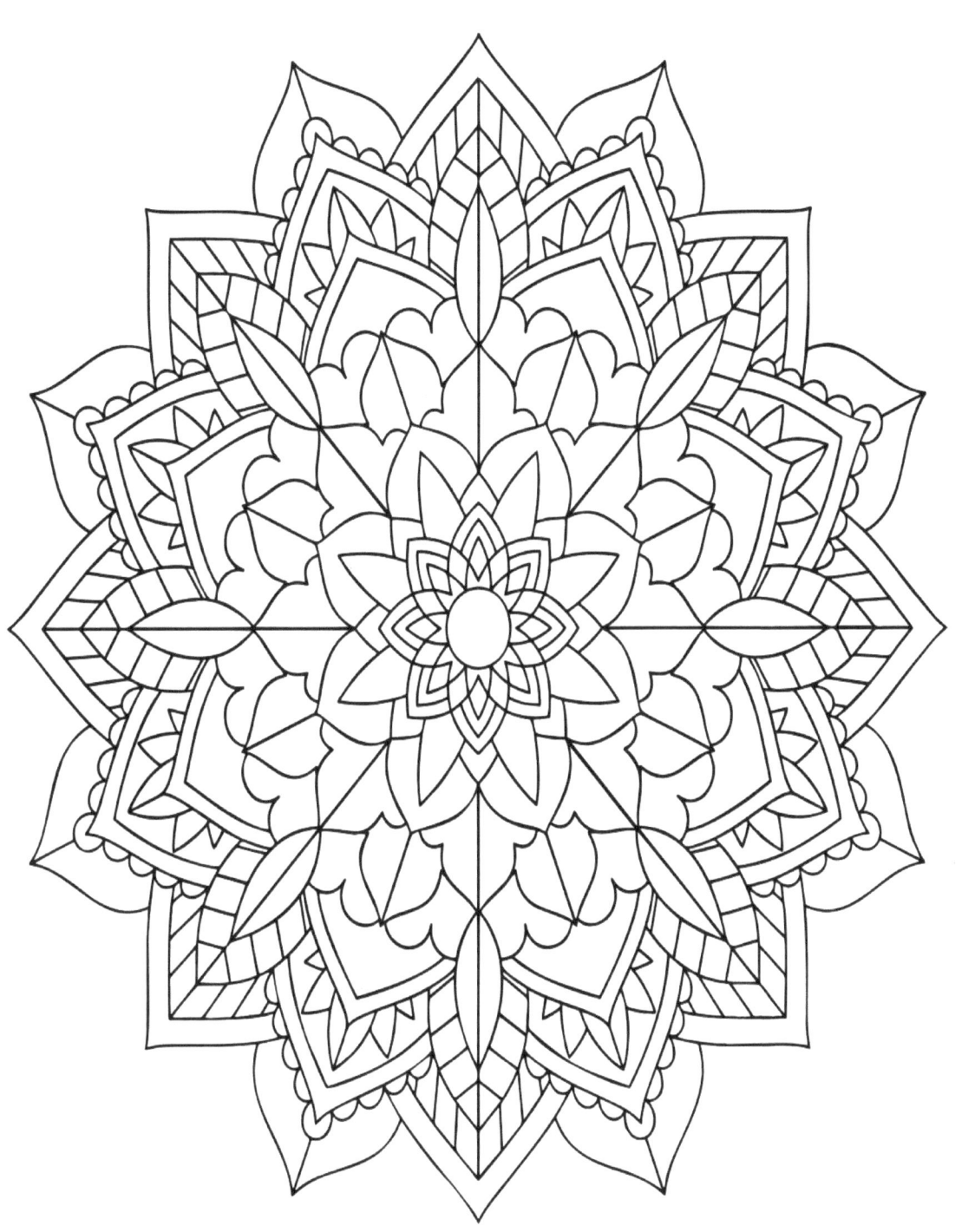

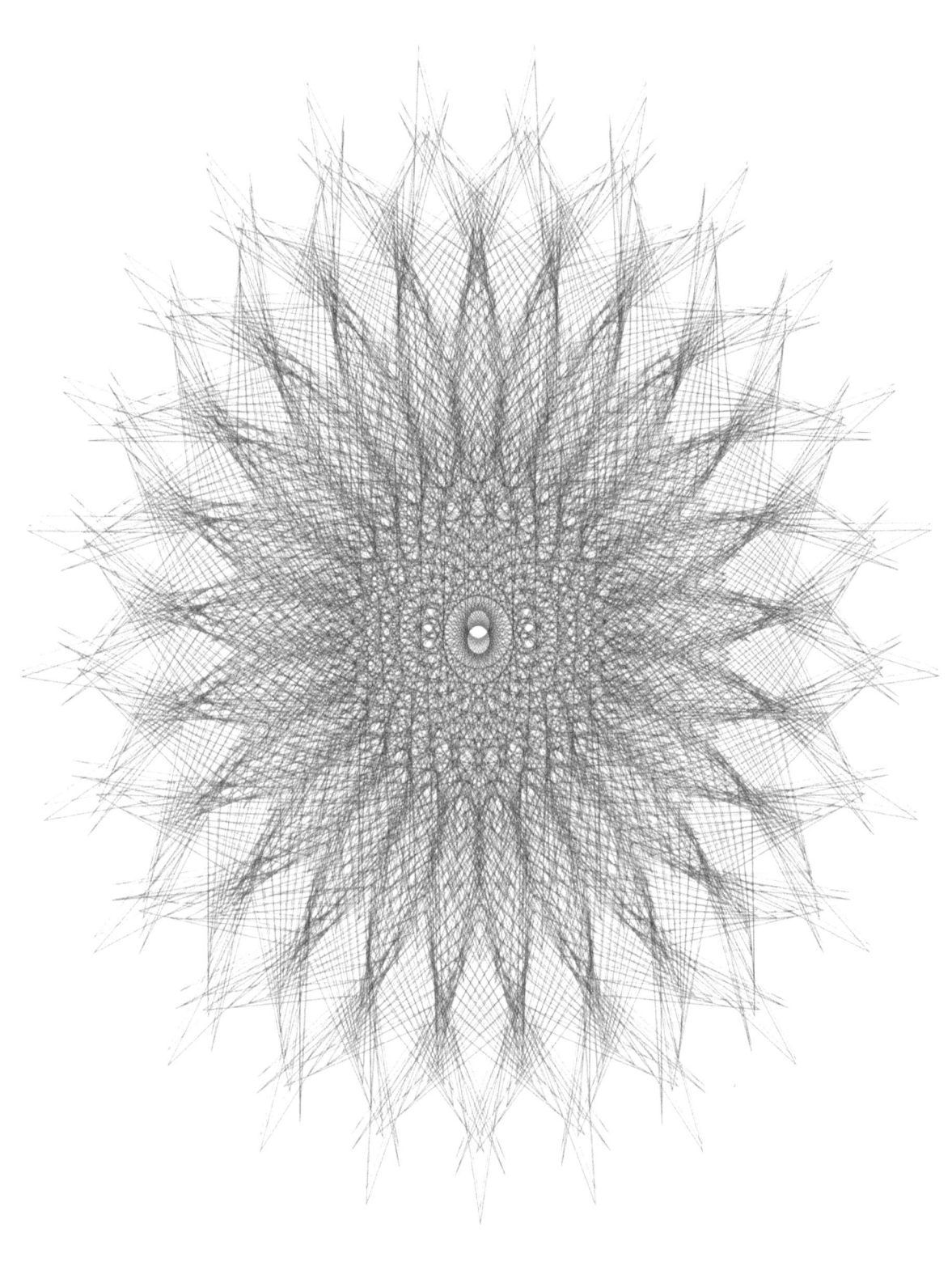

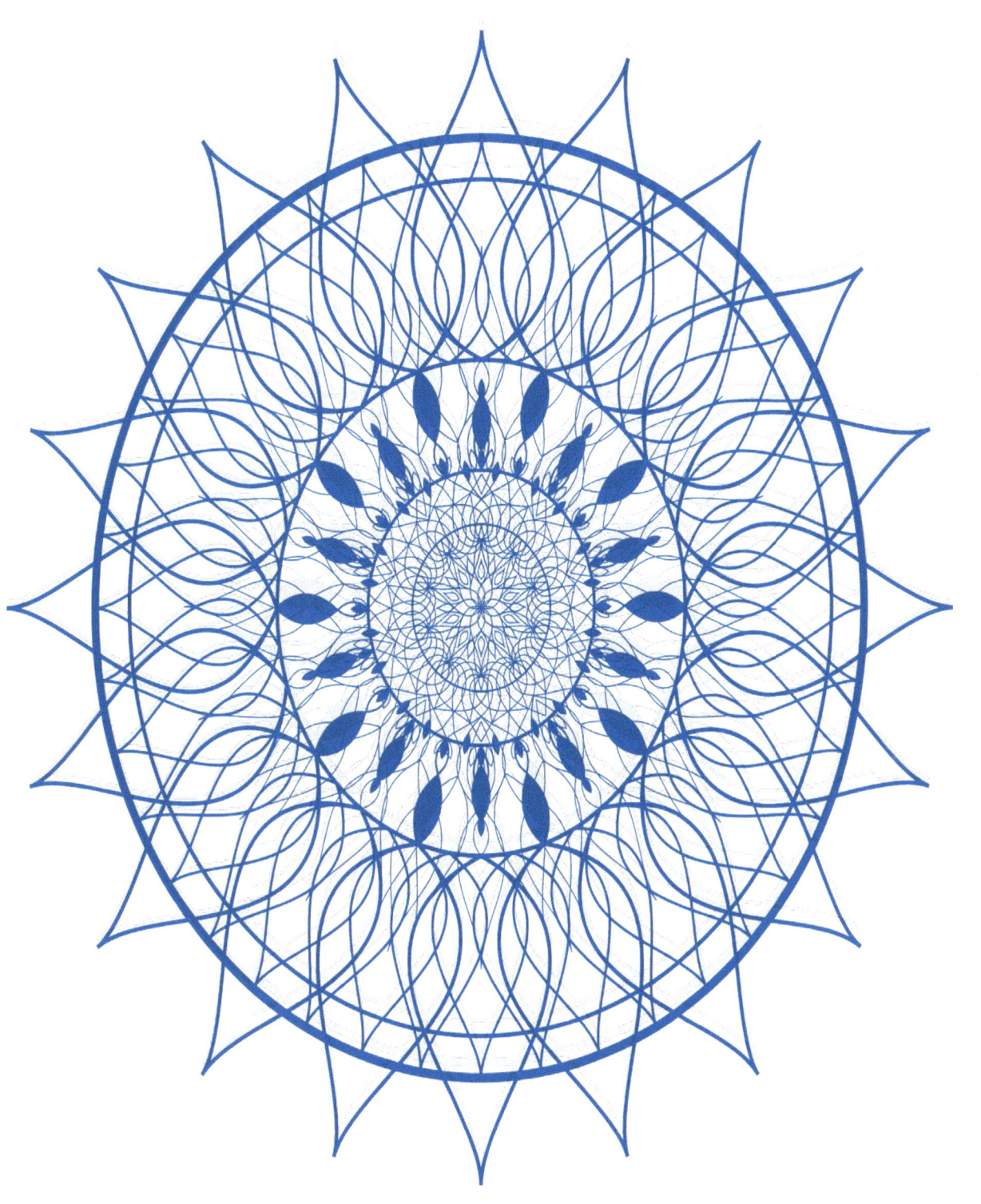

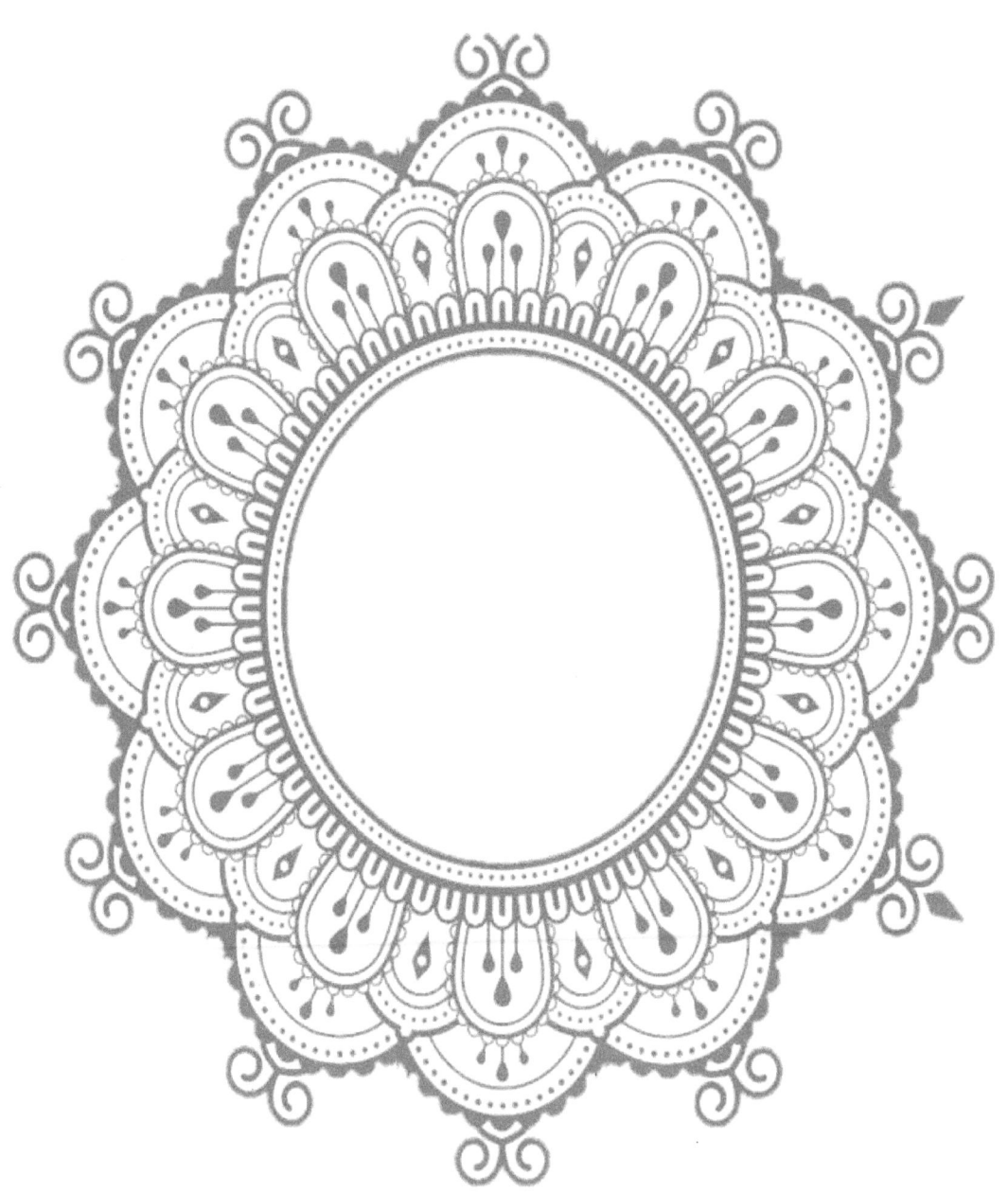

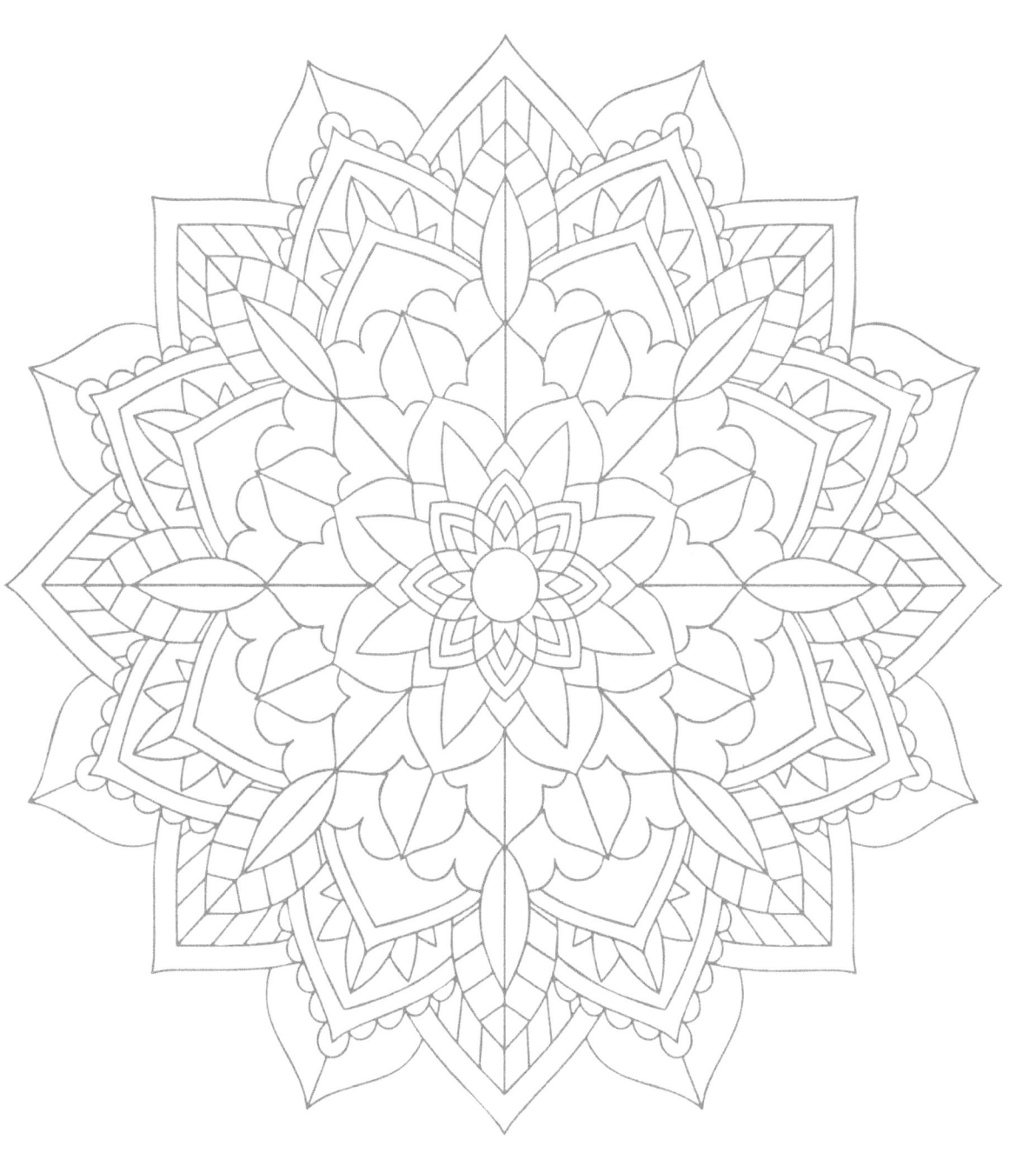

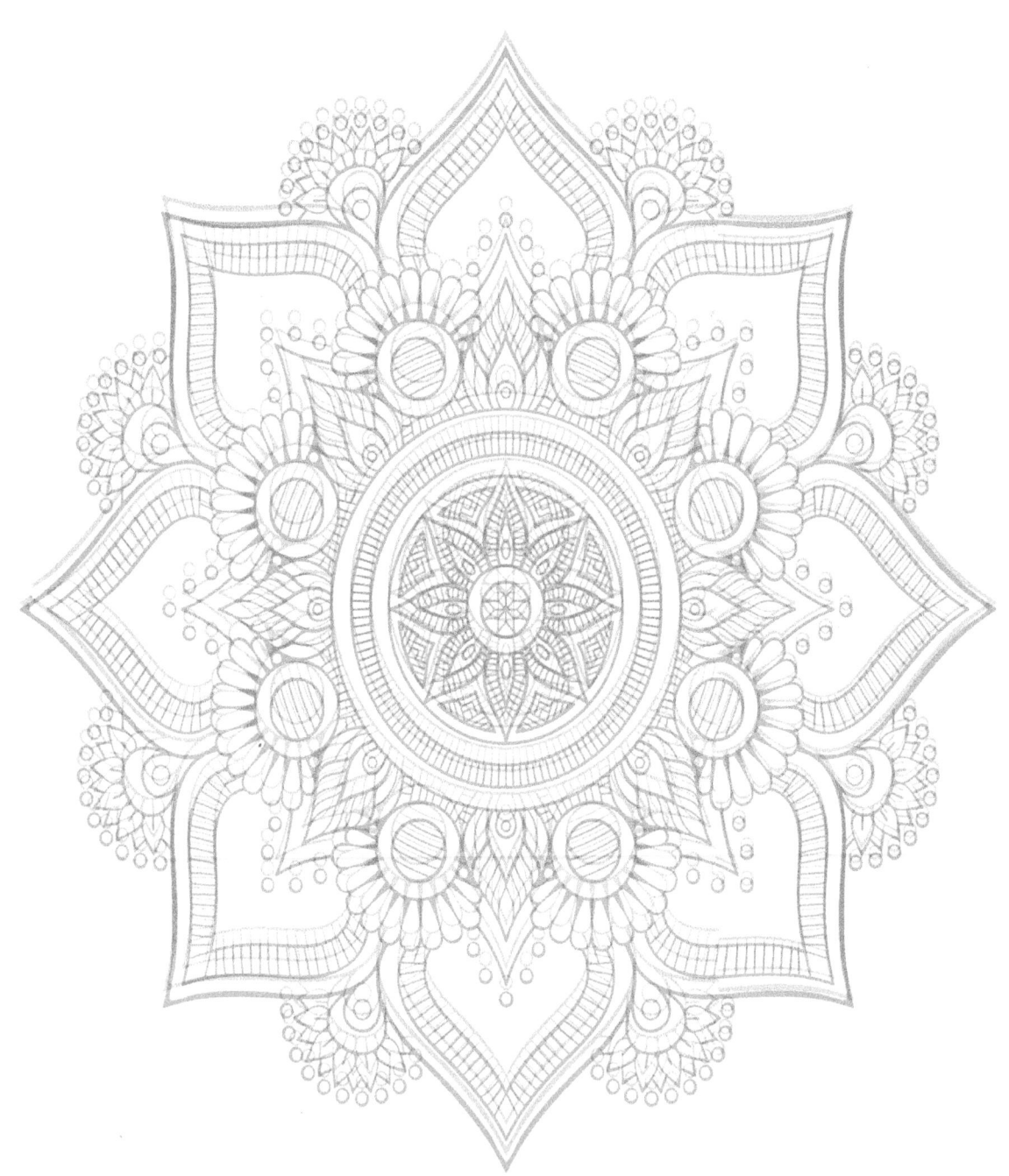

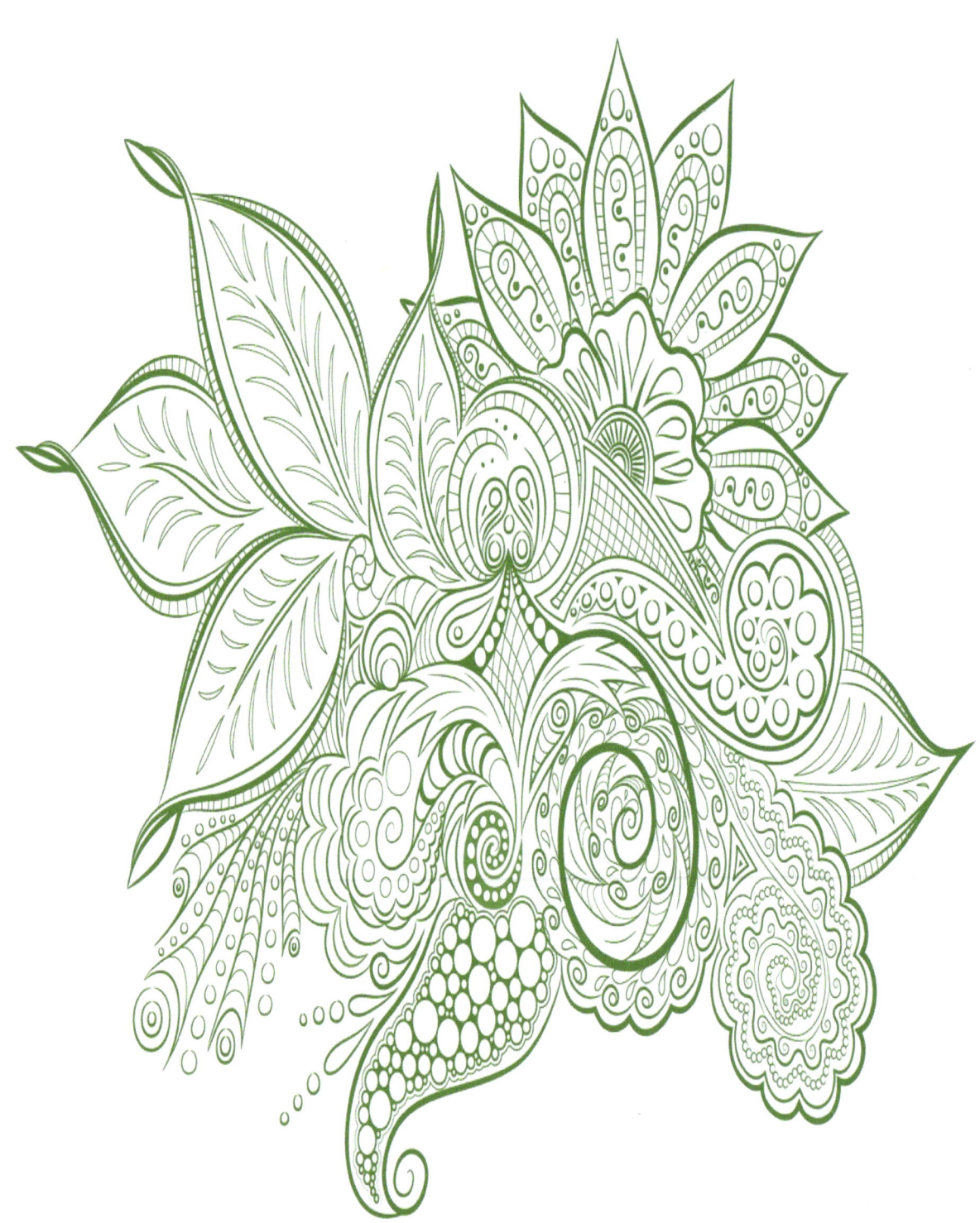

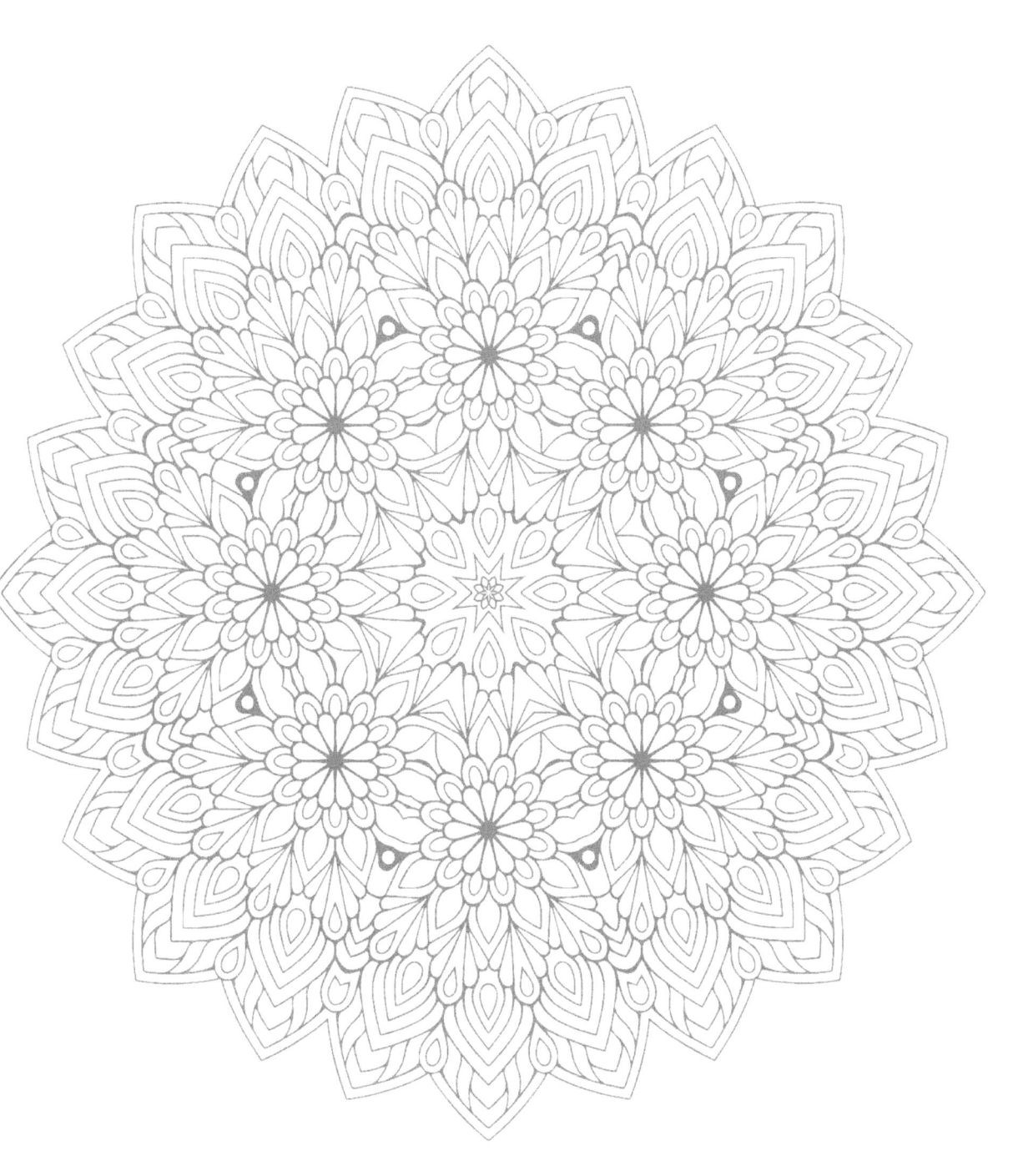

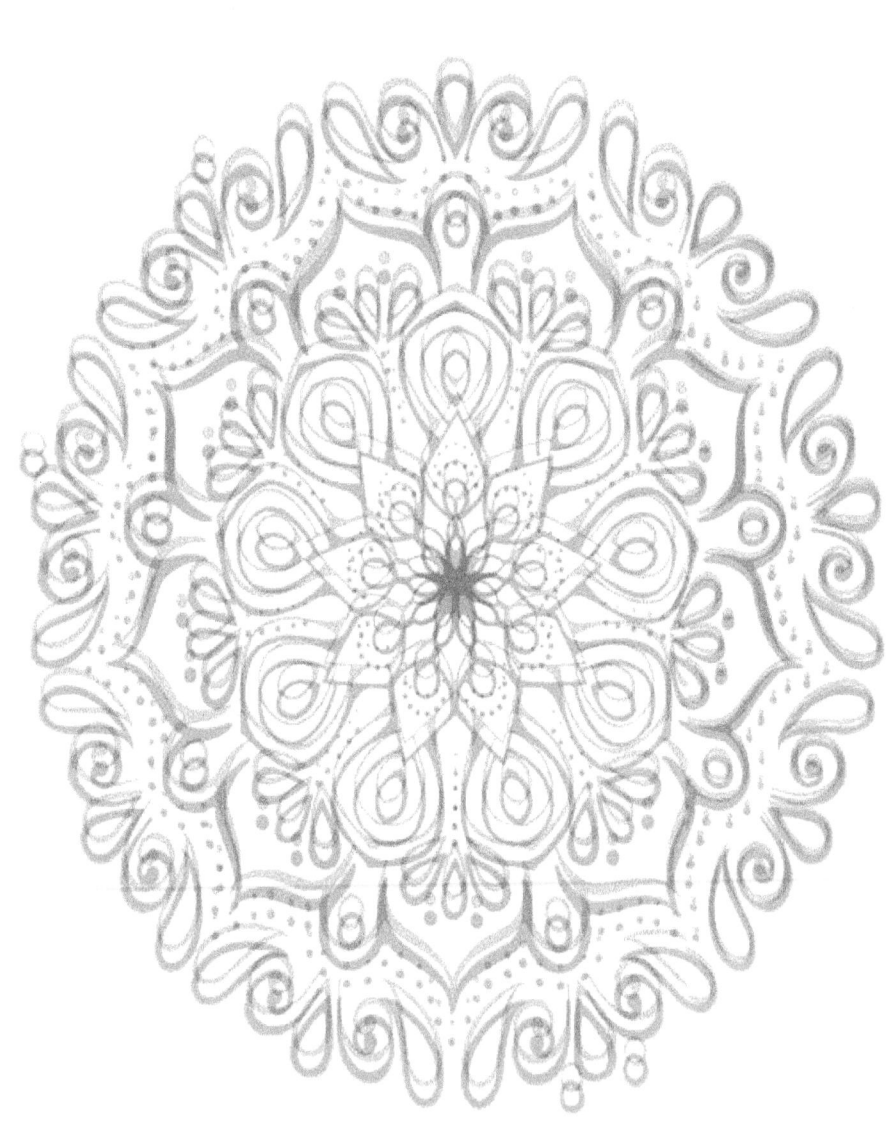

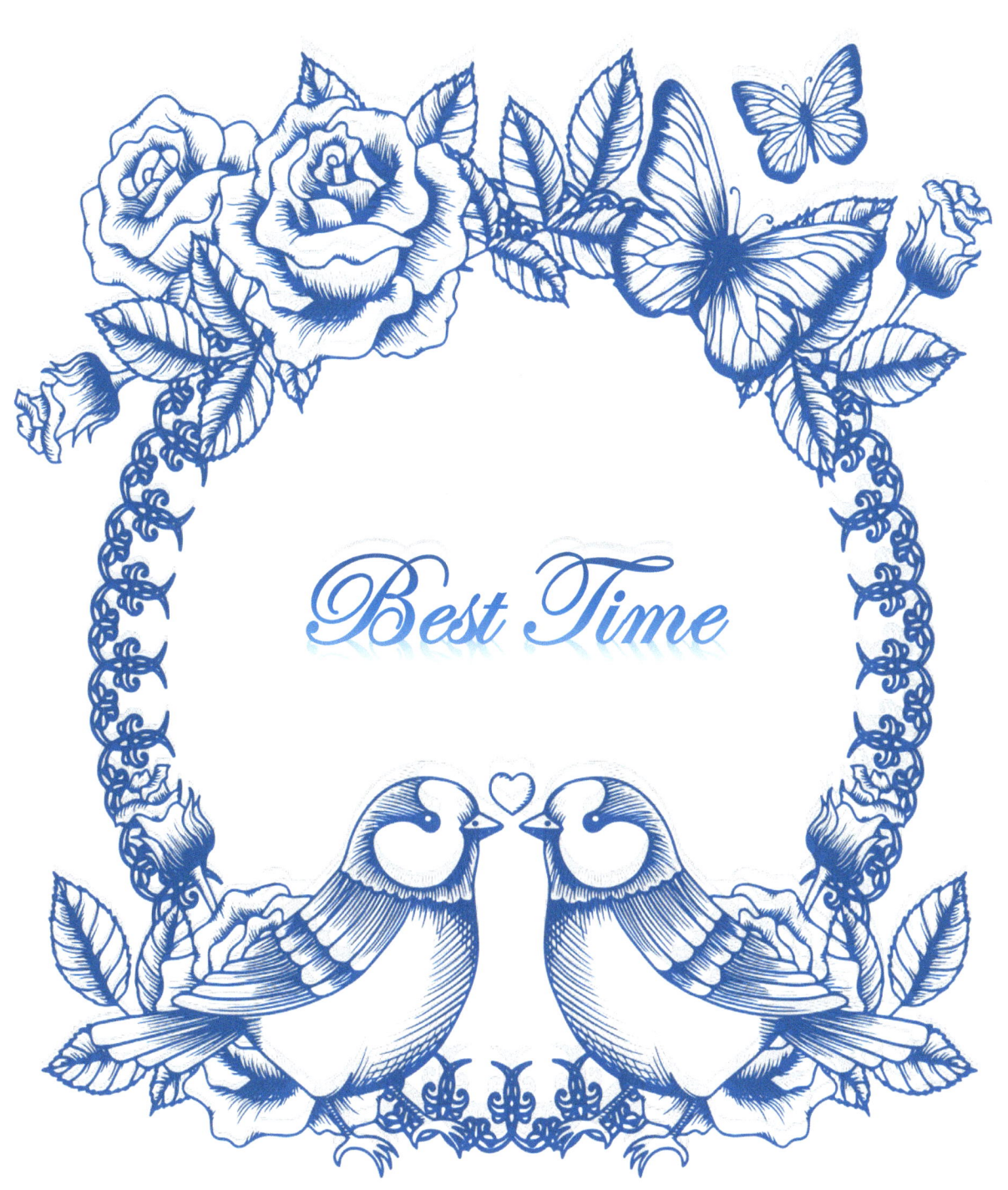

The main circle shape of the mandala is filled with a variety of geometric shapes and symbols, which are often repeated in symmetrical patterns.

www.ingramcontent.com/pod-product-compliance
Lightning Source LLC
Chambersburg PA
CBHW051944210526
45473CB00006B/2374